The Chaparral
Life on the Scrubby Coast

The Chaparral
Life on the Scrubby Coast

Salvatore Tocci

Watts LIBRARY™

Franklin Watts
A Division of Scholastic Inc.
New York • Toronto • London • Auckland • Sydney
Mexico City • New Delhi • Hong Kong

for Rita, whose stories I miss no matter
how many times I heard them.

Note to readers: Definitions for words in **bold** can be found in the Glossary at the back of this book.

Photographs © 2004: AP/Wide World Photos: 54 (Daryl Sullivan/The Daily Times); Bruce Coleman Inc.: 45 (Larry Allan), 25 (Julie Eggers), 22 (Arthur M. Greene); Corbis Images/Christies Images: 46; Dembinsky Photo Assoc.: 23 (Mary Clay), cover (Ed Kanze); Peter Arnold Inc.: 52 (Martin Harvey), 10, 11 (Walter H. Hodge); Photo Researchers, NY: 34 (Bill Bachman), 42 (Nigel J. Dennis), 14 (Dennis Flaherty), 50 (C. Clem Haagner), 33 (Tom McHugh), 37 (Earl Scott), 20, 36 (Dan Suzio), 2 (Karl Weidmann), 41 (Art Wolfe), 6 (Kent Wood); Robertstock.com/R. Krubner: 18, 19; TRIP Photo Library: 17 (M. Gleeson), 5 right, 26 (S. Maxwell), 16 (F. Pirson), 31, 38 (Eric Smith); Visuals Unlimited Inc.: 32, 49 (John D. Cunningham), 8, 29 (Ken Lucas), 5 left, 40 (S. Maslowski), 44 (Rob & Ann Simpson).

The photograph on the cover shows an area of the chaparral in the Victoria Coast of Australia. The photograph opposite the cover page shows the chaparral in southern Venezuela, South America.

Library of Congress Cataloging-in-Publication Data

Tocci, Salvatore.
    The chaparral : life on the scrubby coast / Salvatore Tocci.
       v. cm. — (Watts library)
    Includes bibliographical references and index.
    Contents: The world's smallest biome — Chaparral fires — Plants of the chaparral — Animals of the chaparral — A changed biome.
    ISBN 0-531-12303-0 (lib. bdg.)   0-531-16671-6 (pbk.)
    1. Chaparral ecology—Juvenile literature. [1. Chaparral. 2. Chaparral ecology. 3. Ecology.] I. Title. II. Series.
QH541.5.C5T63 2003
577.3'8—dc22

2003016574

Contents

Lightning may start a fire that can spread quickly through a chaparral.

Fire on the Mountain

One day in the summer of 1977, a park ranger named Bob Doyle saw lightning strike Mount Diablo, which is located in a state park near San Francisco, California. A fire soon broke out and quickly spread throughout the park. The fire raged for five days before it was finally put out. More than 6,000 acres (2,430 hectares) of land in Mount Diablo State Park had been burned.

Back in 1977, every effort was made to put out a park fire as soon as it started.

Today, not only are park fires allowed to burn, they are deliberately started by specially trained park employees. These fires are allowed to burn under carefully controlled conditions and close supervision. In California alone, about 30,000 acres (12,150 ha) in state parks are burned deliberately each year.

One goal of these controlled burns, or **prescribed fires**, is the reduction of the amount of dead wood and brush that accumulates over the years. This material can serve as fuel for a wildfire that can easily get out of control. In other words, prescribed fires are set to halt the spread of a wildfire that would cause widespread damage. In 1992, a wildfire's spread in Mount Diablo State Park was partially stopped when it entered an area that was treated by a prescribed fire the previous year.

Prescribed fires are occasionally started in Mount Diablo State Park for another reason. These fires help maintain the plants that grow there. In turn, these plants support a variety of animal life.

From the summit of Mount Diablo, you can see some 200 miles (320 kilometers) in every direction.

Low trees and shrubs are common in a chaparral.

Chapter One

The World's Smallest Biome

Scientists divide Earth into different geographic areas, called **biomes**, based on such environmental factors as temperature and precipitation. A biome is a unique geographic area with certain environmental conditions that determine the kinds of plants and animals that can live there. With the exception of the ocean, all of the biomes are on land.

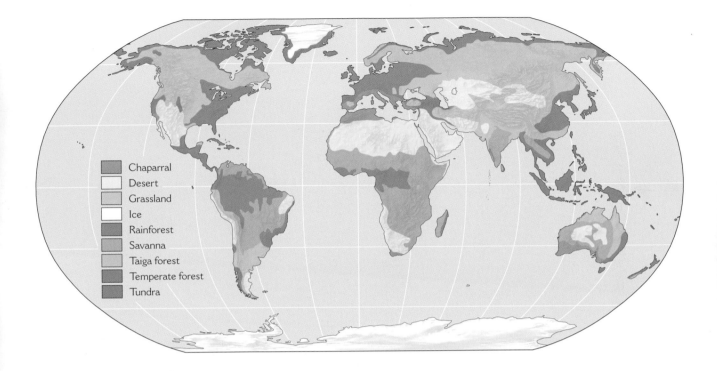

Chaparral
Desert
Grassland
Ice
Rainforest
Savanna
Taiga forest
Temperate forest
Tundra

Mount Diablo State Park is located in a biome known as a **chaparral**. The chaparral is the smallest land biome. Chaparral is a biome in which the winters are mild and wet, and the summers are hot and dry. Only plants and animals that can survive these conditions are found in chaparral. Like all biomes, chaparral can be found in various places on Earth where these conditions exist. In the United States, a chaparral biome stretches from southern Oregon through California. Chaparral biomes also exist along coastal regions of the Mediterranean Sea, southwestern Australia, the southern tip of South Africa, and Chile.

Not One Biome

Antarctica is the only place on Earth that does not have a biome.

Hot Summers and Mild Winters

Two tropical high pressure areas circle Earth. One is found at 30 degrees north latitude. The other is found at 30 degrees south latitude. These two high pressure areas cause a hot, dry climate that is typical of a desert biome.

Chaparrals are found slightly north of the northern high pressure area and slightly south of the southern high pressure area. Because chaparrals are close to these high pressure areas, their summers are hot and dry. Temperatures can climb higher than 100° Fahrenheit (38° Celsius) during the day, just as they do in a desert. During the summer, only a trace of moisture can be found in the air.

Chaparrals have mild winter temperatures because they are close to the tropical high pressure areas. Although the temperature can drop to freezing, it averages between 50° F and 60° F (10° C and 15° C).

In addition, a chaparral is always found in an area that borders an ocean or large sea. Being near a large body of water makes for a wet winter. The average yearly precipitation, which usually falls as rain, is 10–25 inches (25–60 centimeters). In the Northern Hemisphere, most of the rainfall is received between November and April. February is usually the rainiest month. In 1998, almost 11 inches (28 cm) of rain fell during the first week of February in a California chaparral. In the Southern Hemisphere, the rainfall is received mostly between May and September. July is usually the rainiest month.

A Biome With Different Names

In California, a chaparral biome is found on the lower western slopes of the Sierra Nevada, which are as high as 14,000 feet (4,200 meters). In winter, the peaks of these mountains are covered with snow. At the base of the mountains, the shrubs are among the densest found in any chaparral in the world.

In Australia, the chaparral is called **mallee scrub** after a type of small tree that is common in this biome. In many areas,

A chaparral biome is found at the western base of the Sierra Nevada in California.

The Chaparral and Chaps

The word *chaparral* comes from the Mexican word *chaparro*, which means "scrub oak." Scrub oak is a short tree commonly found in this biome. During the 1940s and 1950s, many Hollywood movies about the Wild West were filmed in the California chaparral. Cowboys were often shown riding their horses across the chaparral. The leathery coverings they wore to protect their legs from the thorny plants are called chaps, which comes from the word *chaparral*.

the mallee scrub has been cleared to make way for farms. One of the few places in Australia where the chaparral has been left largely untouched is a small island located south of the mainland. This is Kangaroo Island, which is named after its most famous animal inhabitants. Standing on Kangaroo Island, a person can look for miles in all directions and see nothing but chaparral, consisting of flat plains with thickets of low trees and clumps of tall shrubs.

Around the Mediterranean, the chaparral is called **maquis**, after a type of shrub that is common in this biome. Like the animals in all chaparrals, those that live in a maquis must be able to survive dry summers and wet winters. In addition, these animals must be able to climb the jagged, rocky hills that make up much of the landscape in this area.

In South Africa, the chaparral is called **fynbos**. More than eight thousand types of plants grow there, including about six thousand that are not found anywhere else on Earth. However, few trees grow in the fynbos. Plants that grow in this

chaparral include the proteas, which produces large, colorful flowers. Florists often use protea plants as centerpieces in exotic arrangements.

In Chile, the chaparral is known as **matorral**, from the Spanish word *mata*, which means "shrub." Most shrubs and trees in the matorral have tough, thick leaves that burn easily but can survive droughts. Beech trees dominate the matorral. Cactus plants are much more common in the matorral than in chaparral biomes found in other parts of the world. Unlike most chaparral plants, cacti are not well adapted to survive a fire. However, fires in the matorral are far less common than they are in other areas of chaparral. As a result, cacti can thrive in the Chilean matorral. Although fires occur less frequently, much of the landscape of the matorral is strikingly similar to the chaparral biome of California.

Challenging Conditions

The soil in a chaparral is usually shallow, rocky, and poor in many **nutrients**. Nutrients are substances, such as minerals, that living things need to survive. In addition, the soil is dry during the summer, when rainfall is limited. Even in winter, the soil can hold moisture only for a short time. Despite these challenges, many types of plants grow in a chaparral.

However, chaparral plants do not grow very tall because of the poor soil conditions. Even the trees do not grow much higher than 10 feet (3 m). These plants also face another challenge—fire. Because the chaparral is dry, the brush that accumulates over the years acts as fuel for a wildfire. At times, the fires can get out of control and take days or even weeks to extinguish.

Many chaparral plants produce colorful flowers.

Fires can quickly get out of control in a chaparral.

Chapter Two

Chaparral Fires

Fires on a chaparral are inevitable. Over the years, dead vegetation from the trees and shrubs accumulates. During the summer months, this dead vegetation becomes very dry and turns into a perfect fuel for a fire. All that is needed to start a fire is a source of ignition. Lightning is one source. Fires on a chaparral are also accidentally started by campfires that are not completely extinguished or by matches and cigarettes that are carelessly tossed into the brush.

In 1991, a fire destroyed more than three thousand homes in the California chaparral.

The Santa Ana Winds

The fires that occur in the California chaparral are particularly dangerous. These fires can spread quickly and get out of control because of strong winds that fan the flames. Scientists have uncovered evidence that fires have occurred regularly in the California chaparral for more than five hundred years. Every twenty to thirty years, strong winds have caused these fires to spread across this biome. Like hurricanes, these fires have grown to such size and strength that they have earned names based on where they happened. These include the Hume Fire of 1956, the Wright Fire of 1970, and the Piuma Fire of 1985.

The Old Topanga Fire of 1993 occurred near Malibu, California. This community borders the Pacific Ocean and covers about 45,000 acres (18,225 ha), which is mostly chaparral. Malibu is home to many movie and television stars. The Old Topanga Fire destroyed some of their homes. The fire caused over $200 million in property damage.

The Old Topanga Fire of 1993 was the most destructive. On November 1, 1993, a region of high pressure was located over the area to the east of southern California. At the same time, a low pressure area was located over southern California. The difference in pressure between these two areas caused hot desert air from Nevada and Arizona to blow west and across southern California. The winds became stronger, turning into what the early Spanish settlers called the Santa Ana winds. The next day, winds were averaging 20 to 40 miles (32 to 64 kilometers) per hour, with gusts reaching 60 miles (96 km) per hour. Everyone in the southern California chaparral area knew that conditions were perfect for a fire.

On November 2, a report came in that a fire had started near a water tower on the chaparral. By the time the first fire engine arrived, smoke was visible more than 0.5 mile (1 km) from the water tower. Within an hour after the fire had started, nearly 1,000 acres (405 ha) of chaparral were burning. Winds blew the flames 200 feet (60 m) into the air. The fire burned for about thirty-six hours before it ran out of fuel when it reached the Pacific Ocean. In that short time, the fire killed

three people, injured twenty-one civilians and 565 fire fighters, and burned more than 16,000 acres (6,480 ha) of chaparral.

Fighting Fire With Fire

People have long known that the dry vegetation that accumulates over time makes the chaparral a prime setting for a fire. The first people to settle the California chaparral were a tribe of American Indians known as the Chumash. The Chumash lived mainly along the coast, scattered among approximately 150 separate villages. They got most of their food from the sea. To supplement their diet, they traveled inland to the chaparral. There they hunted deer and other wild game. They also gathered seeds and berries from the plants.

Soon after they first settled in the chaparral, the Chumash became aware of how easily fires could start because of the dry

Chapter Three

Plants of the Chaparral

The kinds of plants found in a chaparral depend on the particular environment in which they grow. For example, some chaparral areas in the Mediterranean region have rocky soil that is very poor in nutrients. Shrubs with woody branches are scattered throughout these areas. In contrast, the soil in other Mediterranean chaparral areas is less rocky and contains somewhat more nutrients. This region supports a wider variety of plants, including small oaks and olive trees.

Adaptations

In any environment, every **organism**, or living thing, has a set of conditions under which it will best survive and grow. The dry, hot summers and the wet, mild winters of the chaparral are ideal conditions for certain kinds of plants. These plants have the **adaptations** that are necessary for survival in these conditions. An adaptation is a feature that increases an organism's chances of survival.

Despite their differences, all chaparral plants share certain adaptations. For example, they all are adapted to survive the hot, dry summers. They must have adaptations that allow them to obtain what little water is available during the dry season. One such adaptation can be seen in their roots, which usually spread out wide to capture as much surface water as

The Mediterranean Chaparral

In contrast to the maquis, Mediterranean chaparral with poorer soil is called garigue.

Dangerous Plant Oils

Two chaparral plants whose leaves secrete oil are poison ivy and poison oak. This oil is a clear, sticky substance that causes an allergic reaction in most people and causes a red, itchy rash. The oil can stick to almost anything, especially a person's skin. The first time a person comes in contact with the oil, an allergic reaction may not occur. However, those who are sensitive will develop a rash on any subsequent encounter. Scientists estimate that as many as 75 percent of people are allergic to the oil.

People who are very sensitive to the oil do not even have to come in contact with the plant to feel its effects. The oil can be carried by the wind or by smoke from a fire. If the oil is inhaled, a person may develop a rash inside the mouth or digestive tract. This is a concern for firefighters fighting a blaze in burning chaparral.

possible after winter rains. Their roots also grow deep into the soil to absorb groundwater during the dry season.

Chaparral plants must also be able to conserve water. Their leaves are usually small, narrow, and needlelike. As a result, they do not lose much water through evaporation. To conserve water, the leaves of many chaparral plants are also covered with a waxy or oily substance. One plant with this adaptation is the chamise. The waxy substance on its leaves is highly flammable. Whenever the leaves of a chamise plant burn, they produce a hot flame and black smoke. This is one reason fires burn so intensely and travel so quickly through a chaparral.

The chamise plant burns easily and quickly because of the waxy substance on its leaves.

Not surprisingly, chaparral plants can be grouped according to the way they interact with fire. The chamise is only one of a group of many chaparral plants that are highly flammable. Other types of plants that grow in chaparral do not burn as easily.

Fire-Retardant Plants

There are no fire-resistant plants. If a fire burns long and hot enough, any plant will be consumed by the flames. However, some chaparral plants are fire-retardant, which means they are less combustible than others. These fire-retardant plants can escape permanent damage from a fire, especially one that moves quickly through a chaparral.

Unlike chamise, some chaparral plants do not have any wax or oils that will readily catch on fire. In addition, these plants have little or no wood to sustain a fire even if one starts. An example of such a fire-retardant plant is saltbush, a shrub that thrives in the Australian chaparral. Saltbushes are well adapted to grow in salty, rocky soil that does not retain much water. Often, they are the only plants that can tolerate these conditions. Saltbush shrubs have grayish-green leaves that are covered with tiny hairs. These hairs secrete excess salt absorbed from the soil. Excreting salt helps the plant retain water.

Like other chaparral plants, saltbush carries out a special type of **photosynthesis**. Photosynthesis is the process through which plants make sugars. Photosynthesis is a chemical process that stops when the temperature gets too hot, as it

Interesting Names

Other fire-retardant chaparral plants include snow in summer and lemonade berry.

30

does in the chaparral during the daylight hours in summer. However, the type of photosynthesis that occurs in saltbush plants can operate at these higher temperatures, although it happens at a slower rate.

Another fire-retardant chaparral plant is the ice plant. This plant grows low to the ground, has shallow roots, and produces colorful flowers in the spring. During the wet winter

The Chumash harvested the seeds and leaves of saltbush shrubs for food.

31

Ice plants provide a colorful ground cover.

months, ice plants soak up and retain water. All this water helps make the plant fire-retardant during the dry season.

Fire-Adapted Plants

Even such highly flammable plants as the chamise have ways of surviving fires. These plants are said to be fire-adapted. While its stems and leaves are usually destroyed by fire, a new chamise plant can arise from buds that are buried in the soil. These buds are called **lignotubers**. They are deep enough in the soil to remain undamaged by the effects of intense heat.

Lignotubers are a major factor in the survival of the California chaparral, where chamise plants make up nearly 70 percent of the vegetation. Much of this vegetation is destroyed by the frequent brush fires that occur during the fall because of the Santa Ana winds. Without their lignotubers, the chamise plants would not be able to reappear on the chaparral after a fire.

Another fire-adapted chaparral plant is the hollyleaf cherry tree. Like most chaparral plants, this tree usually does not grow very tall. However, with the proper conditions, and if there are no fires, this tree can grow as tall as 25 feet (8 m). Such a tree may be hundreds of years old.

As it name suggests, the hollyleaf cherry tree has shiny, dark green leaves, just like a holly bush. The hollyleaf cherry produces clusters of creamy white flowers in the spring. Later in the year, the tree produces bright red berries that have a tart taste. If a fire does destroy the tree, buds attached to the stump that remains will start to sprout. Within four years, they will produce a hollyleaf tree that is 4 to 5 feet (1.2 to 1.5 m) tall.

The eucalyptus tree, which is commonly found in the Australian chaparral, is another fire-adapted plant. Eucalyptus leaves are rich in oils, which are extracted for use in perfumes, cough drops, and medicines. However, in the chaparral, these

The hollyleaf cherry is known as a stump sprouter because its can sprout a new tree from its stump after a fire.

Eucalyptus trees can survive poor soil, drought, and fire.

The Tallest Tree

A fallen eucalyptus tree in Australia is believed to have once stood more than 490 feet (150 m) tall.

oils serve as fuel for fires. When a fire breaks out, the thick, tough bark of a eucalyptus tree peels off in layers. As a result, the core of the tree is protected from damage. The heat causes new buds to form and sprout after the fire goes out. Large amounts of nutrients that have been stored by the tree are used by the developing buds.

Another adaptation to fire is seen in the seeds of chaparral plants. For example, manzanita seeds remain underground for a long time, perhaps for hundreds of years, without ever sprouting. Buried in the soil, the seeds are protected from fire. Whenever a fire does destroy the vegetation, the manzanita seeds sprout and give rise to new plants.

Fire-Dependent Plants

Without fire, some plants might become less numerous in a chaparral. Such plants include a variety of pine trees. These pine trees grow in and near **montane**, which is a type of chaparral found on mountain slopes at 3,000 to 9,000 feet (900 to 2,700 m) above sea level.

Pine trees produce cones that contain seeds. In most pine trees, the cones open when mature and release the seeds, which fall to the ground. If the soil contains enough moisture, the seeds will sprout to produce new pine trees.

In contrast, pine trees of the montane have some cones that remain closed, even when they are mature. If the cones remain closed, the seeds remain inside them and are not able to produce new pine trees to replace those that die. However, when a fire occurs, its heat forces the cones open, releasing the seeds to start another generation.

Some chaparral plants do not respond to the heat of a fire. Instead, the smoke from the fire triggers a reaction. The seeds of some South African shrubs start to grow only after they have been exposed to smoke. The seeds of some flowering

The Coulter pine produces the largest cone of any pine tree. The cone can be as long as 14 inches (35 cm).

plants also require smoke to sprout. These include golden eardrops and whispering bells, which produce yellow, bell-shaped flowers. Unless a fire has occurred in the recent past, these flowering plants may never appear in a chaparral.

Just after a fire, all that can be seen are the ashes and charred remains of the vegetation that once thrived. It is hard to imagine that anything will ever grow there again. However, new life will begin to appear within several months after a fire.

Following a wet winter, the next spring will find the chaparral covered with a dazzling variety of colorful flowers. These will include golden daisies, orange poppies, red paintbrush, crimson fire lilies, bronze snapdragons, and purple lilacs. After a few years, many of these colorful plants will be replaced by grasses and shrubs, such as the chamise and manzanita. In about ten years, the chaparral will look much like it did before the fire. Even the animals that were displaced by the fire will have returned.

Colorful flowering plants are the first to appear in a chaparral after a fire.

A kangaroo hops across an Australian chaparral.

Chapter Four

Animals of the Chaparral

The chaparral is the world's smallest biome and is often bordered by one or more other biomes, such as deserts. As a result, most of the animals found in a chaparral also inhabit other biomes. These animals include mice, rabbits, squirrels, snakes, lizards, coyotes, rats, deer, birds, and foxes.

No matter how many different biomes it inhabits, an animal must be adapted to survive the hot, dry summers in the chaparral. The San Joaquin kit fox is

Fully grown, the kit fox has an average body length of 20 inches (50 cm) and weighs about 5 pounds (2 kilograms).

Do Not Disturb

A rattlesnake will attack a human only when it is alarmed or surprised.

such an animal. This fox lives in the California chaparral and in grassland biomes. The fox hunts at night and seeks relief from the daytime heat by taking shelter in a den it digs in the ground. The fox's ears are rather large for its body size. They act like radiators, giving off excess heat and cooling the fox. The fur and hair on the pads of its paws protect the fox from the heat of the soil.

Snakes are another animal found in the chaparral and in other biomes, especially the desert. The most common snake in the California chaparral is the rattlesnake, which hunts at night and feeds mainly on small animals, such as mice and rats.

Special structures on each side of the rattlesnake's snout can sense the body heat given off by another animal.

Only in the Mallee

Unlike the kit fox and rattlesnake, some animals are found only in the chaparral. An example is the western grey kangaroo, also known as the mallee kangaroo because it lives only in the mallee scrub of Australia. The males can grow to be 7 feet (2 m) tall and to weigh as much as 120 pounds (55 kg). Females are both shorter and lighter. Like all kangaroos, the western grey kangaroo has a thick tail to help it balance and strong hind legs for standing upright and hopping. Normally, the western grey kangaroo will jump about 5 feet (1.5 m), but it can leap 30 feet (9 m) or more whenever it is moving fast.

The western grey kangaroo is also known as the black-faced kangaroo because of the dark color of its muzzle.

The western grey kangaroo can go for long periods without drinking water. Its long ears help release excess body heat to keep it cool during hot weather. The western grey kangaroo is also nocturnal, hunting during the late afternoon and night and resting during the day. This animal feeds on grasses and shrubs.

Only in the Fynbos and Maquis

Another animal that lives solely in the chaparral is the grysbok, which is a small antelope that inhabits the South African fynbos. The grysbok is a small animal, measuring about 20 inches (50 cm) high at the shoulders and weighing about 25 pounds (11 kg). Its small size allows the animal to

The grysbok hides in chaparral vegetation to avoid being eaten by its predators, which include the lion and the leopard.

move easily through the thick vegetation that covers the fynbos. The vegetation also serves to hide the grysbok, which lies flat on the ground with its neck outstretched whenever it senses danger. Like most chaparral animals, the grysbok is nocturnal, eating vegetation at night and resting during the day. The grysbok can also go for long periods of time without drinking water.

The Mediterranean maquis is home to a wild sheep known as the mouflon. This animal is thought to be an ancestor of all modern sheep breeds. At one time, the mouflon lived throughout much of Europe. Today, however, this animal is found only on the islands of Sardinia and Corsica. The animals live in groups of twenty to thirty individuals, which roam the maquis looking for grass to eat. The male uses its large,

No Longer Around

Lions and elephants once roamed the fynbos before people built their homes and farms on it.

Feeding Relationships

Feeding relationships in the chaparral, as in all biomes, can be complex. Rarely does one organism depend entirely on another organism for food. Rather, one type of organism eats a variety of other organisms. For example, the California thrasher eats the seeds and fruits of several kinds of plants. In turn, the thrasher may serve as a meal for several other kinds of organisms, including hawks, skunks, foxes, and raccoons. Hawks feed on rabbits and mice as well. Mice, which eat seeds, are eaten by skunks.

Each feeding relationship is usually diagrammed as an arrow going from an organism to the organism it eats. For example, an arrow would be drawn from a hawk to a California thrasher. If all the feeding relationships in a chaparral were shown, the result would be a collection of overlapping lines that resembles a spider's web. For this reason, feeding relationships are known as a food web.

The mouflon's wooly coat protects it from the cold in winter.

heart-shaped horns to protect itself. During the summer, the males live apart from the females and rejoin them in late fall to breed.

The California Chaparral

The California chaparral is the only known home of a bird called the California thrasher. This bird is well adapted to life in the chaparral. Its small size enables it to hide in the dense brush, where it is camouflaged by the brown colors of its body. The thrasher's long, sturdy legs help it run for protection whenever it does venture out from the brush. Its long, curved bill allows it to dig for insects and seeds buried beneath the ground.

Almost all the types of animals found in the California chaparral inhabit other biomes. Many leave the chaparral during the summer heat and return in the fall. Unfortunately, some of those that leave will never return. One such animal is the California grizzly bear. At one time, these bears roamed the chaparral. Fearing that their livestock would be attacked, early settlers shot the grizzly bears on sight. The last California grizzly bear was shot in 1922. Today, the grizzly bear remains only as a symbol on the California state flag.

A California grizzly bear could weigh more than 1,000 pounds (450 kg).

American Indians
depended upon the
chaparral to survive.

Chapter Five

A Changed Biome

Throughout the world, the chaparral has been greatly affected by human activities. The California chaparral is a clear example. For the most part, the Chumash Indians who first inhabited this region did not disturb it. They were not farmers. Rather, they fished, hunted, and gathered the seeds, fruits, and berries of plants they found growing in the chaparral.

However, all this changed when the first Spanish settlers arrived in the 1770s. Rather than depend on chaparral plants for food, these settlers planted crops and raised livestock. To do this, they uprooted the native plants and tilled the soil to make it more suitable for their crops. They also stopped the practice of starting prescribed fires, which they felt posed a danger to their crops and farm animals. As more and more settlers arrived, they began to move into areas of the chaparral that had never been occupied by humans.

Building Homes

About 20,000 Chumash lived in about 150 small villages scattered throughout the California chaparral. Today, this same area is home to more than thirty million people. About 90 percent of these people live in cities. Obviously, millions of homes have been built in and near what was once chaparral. Much of the native vegetation has been cleared to make way for these homes. Only patches of chaparral vegetation remain in what was once an undisturbed biome.

The impact of human settlement on many chaparral animals and plants has been devastating. Today, many of them are endangered or threatened with extinction. More than seventy types of animals in the California chaparral are listed as endangered. These include the California condor, several types of kangaroo rats, the San Joaquin kit fox, the blunt-nosed leopard lizard, and the San Francisco garter snake. Thirteen types of chaparral plants are also endangered, including the Mount Diablo manzanita, fairy lantern, buckwheat, phacelia, jewel flower, and cottonweed plants.

A Big Bird

The California condor is the largest bird of prey in North America.

*More people living in
the chaparral also
means that the chances
of fire are greater.*

Farming the Land

The Mountain Zebra National Park in the Republic of South Africa is home to this animal, which almost became extinct in 1937.

People have changed the chaparral not only by building homes on it but also by converting it into farmland. The South African fynbos shows how agriculture has affected the chaparral. The first European settlers, mostly Dutch, settled in South Africa in the 1600s. As more and more settlers arrived, they turned large areas of fynbos into farmland. As a result, nearly half the fynbos have been replaced by agricultural and grazing land.

Animals that once roamed the fynbos have been forced to live in other biomes. These animals include elephants, lions, buffalos, and zebras. In an effort to save fynbos animals and plants from extinction, the Republic of South Africa has established a large number of game preserves and national parks.

Introducing Non-Native Plants

As humans built their homes and developed their farms in the chaparral, they often did something else that has had a negative impact. They introduced plants that are not normally found in this biome. These plants are referred to as non-native, or alien, plants. Perhaps the most striking effect of the introduction of these alien plants can be seen in the fynbos.

Since the Dutch settlers first starting arriving, more than three hundred types of alien plants have been introduced into the fynbos. Many of these plants, such as pine and eucalyptus trees, are much more flammable than those that normally grow in the fynbos. Not only are they more likely to burn, but these alien plants also produce much more heat when they burn. As a result, the frequency of fires in the fynbos has increased significantly, and the increased heat has caused much more damage to native plants.

These alien plants have also changed soil conditions. Pine and eucalyptus trees have developed into forests that use what little water is available in the fynbos. Even though they are adapted to drought conditions, native chaparral plants cannot survive indefinitely without water.

Extinct Animals

The destruction of the fynbos led to the extinction of the blue antelope and the quagga, which is a relative of the zebra.

In one hour, a worker can cut down more than three hundred alien trees growing in the fynbos.

Aware that the problem could become a major disaster, the South African government has taken steps to preserve the natural fynbos. More than forty thousand people have been hired to cut down as many alien trees as possible. These workers are often transported by helicopter to remote regions where the alien trees have formed forests. Scientists have also introduced a fungus into these forests to kill the alien trees. Fortunately, the fynbos are starting to make a comeback in many areas.

Saving the Chaparral

Efforts are also underway in other parts of the world to save the chaparral from further destruction. When it was first established, the U.S. Forest Service made it a policy to prevent forest fires and to extinguish any fire that did start as quickly as possible. The Forest Service warned people that "One tree can make a million matches, but one match can kill a million trees." Films were shown in schools throughout the country that featured Smokey the Bear, who warned, "Only *you* can prevent forest fires."

In the 1970s, the Forest Service began experimenting with prescribed fires in selected parks. Yet, it still focused on suppressing more than 99 percent of all fires. Its motto continued to be "Put out all fires by 10 AM." However, the goal of preventing and putting out all fires as quickly as possible soon started to change.

Today, both state and national agencies regularly set prescribed fires in the chaparral. Every effort is made to ensure that the fire stays within a designated area. In addition, no fire is started unless weather conditions will assist people in

A forest ranger is starting a prescribed fire to prevent a more serious wildfire from starting in the chaparral.

controlling it. A forest ranger who manages a prescribed fire today is doing exactly what a Chumash Indian first did hundreds of years ago. Both are trying to save the chaparral.

Glossary

adaptation—feature that increases an organism's chance of survival

biome—geographic area in which specific kinds of plants and animals are found

chaparral—biome in which the plants and animals are adapted to hot, dry summers and mild, wet winters

climax community—plants that are found in the final and stable stage of succession

fynbos—name for the chaparral in South Africa

lignotuber—underground bud that can sprout after a fire

mallee scrub—name for the chaparral in Australia

maquis—name for the chaparral in the Mediterranean region

matorral—name for the chaparral in Chile

montane—chaparral vegetation that is found on higher elevations on mountains

nutrient—substance an organism needs to live and grow

organism—living thing

photosynthesis—process by which plants make sugars and other foods

prescribed fire—fire that is deliberately set and closely monitored

succession—gradual change that occurs in the types of living things found in a particular environment

To Find Out More

Books

Cowling, R.M. *Fynbos: South Africa's Unique Floral Kingdom.* Fernwood Press, 1995.

Langeland, Deirdre. *Kangaroo Island: The Story of an Australian Mallee Forest.* Soundprints Corp. Audio, 1998.

Ricciuti, Edward R. *Chaparral (Biomes of the World).* Benchmark Books, 1996.

Organizations and Online Sites

California Native Plant Society
2707 K Street, Suite 1
Sacramento, CA 95816-5113

(916) 447-2677

www.cnps.org/kidstuff/chaparral.htm

This site has information on how plants are adapted to the California chaparral and how fire helps preserve the nature of this biome.

National Wildlife Federation
11100 Wildlife Center Drive
Reston, VA 20190-5362
(703) 438-6000

www.nwf.org/internationalwildlife/1998/fynbos.html

Read a story about twenty members of the Alien Hit Squad, whose mission is to eliminate the enemy. In this case, the enemy consists of American pines and other alien trees that are threatening the plants that normally grow in the fynbos.

Plants of the Chaparral

www.acc.scu.edu/~respinol

Learn more about chaparral plants, including how they deal with low levels of water. You can also get more specific information by clicking on the names of individual plants such as wild cucumber, coyote brush, and sticky monkey flower.

Chaparral: A Forgotten Habitat

www.laep.org/target/units/chaparral/index.html

This site contains an extensive list of plants that are found on the California chaparral.

Chilean Matorral

www.worldwildlife.org/wildworld/profiles/g200/g122.html

Read about the Chilean chaparral and see how this biome is being affected by the increasing number of people moving into this biome.

Mediterranean Plants

www.bbc.co.uk/nature/plants/worldplants/med.shtml

Read about the plants found on the European maquis and garigue and why some of them are not found anyplace else in the world.

A Note on Sources

As the world's smallest biome, the chaparral has not received much attention from book authors. As a result, I had to find much of the information I included in this book from the Internet. While sorting through the materials I came across, my main concern was selecting only reliable sources. This meant focusing on reports, descriptions, summaries, updates, and events found on online sites maintained by state and federal agencies, such as the USDA Forest Service, and environmental organizations, such as the World Wildlife Federation.

—Salvatore Tocci

Index

Numbers in *italics* indicate illustrations.

About the Author

Salvatore Tocci taught high school and college science for almost thirty years. He has a bachelor's degree from Cornell University and a Master of Philosophy degree from The City University of New York.

He has written books that deal with a range of science topics, from biographies about famous scientists to a high school chemistry textbook. He has also traveled throughout the United States to present workshops at national science conventions to show teachers how to emphasize to their students the applications of scientific knowledge to everyday life.

Tocci lives in East Hampton, New York, with his wife Patti. Both retired from teaching, they spend their leisure time traveling and have visited the California chaparral and the Mediterranean maquis. They plan to travel to the Australian mallee scrub in the near future.